ISBN: 9798328248921
Independently published

i

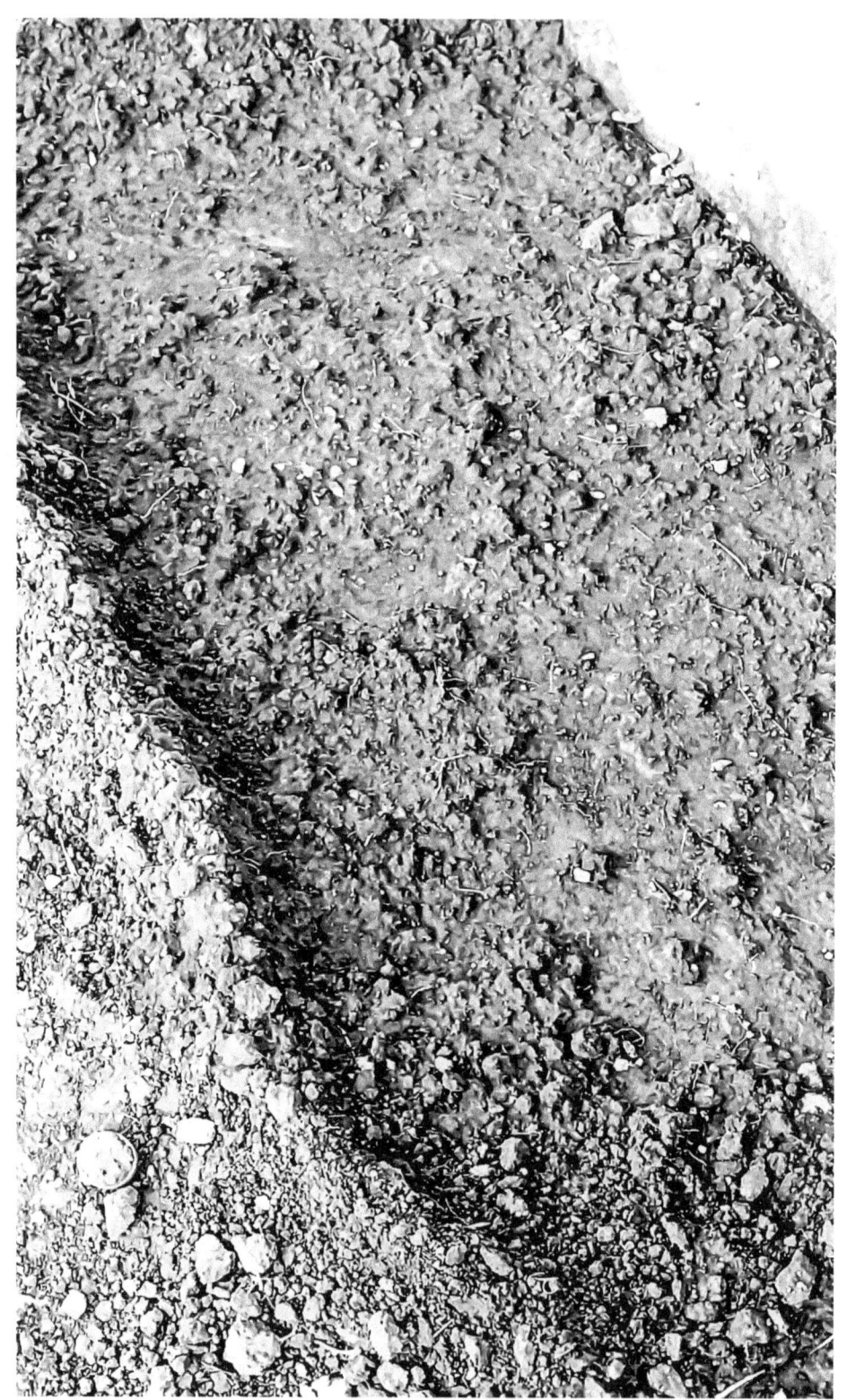

1

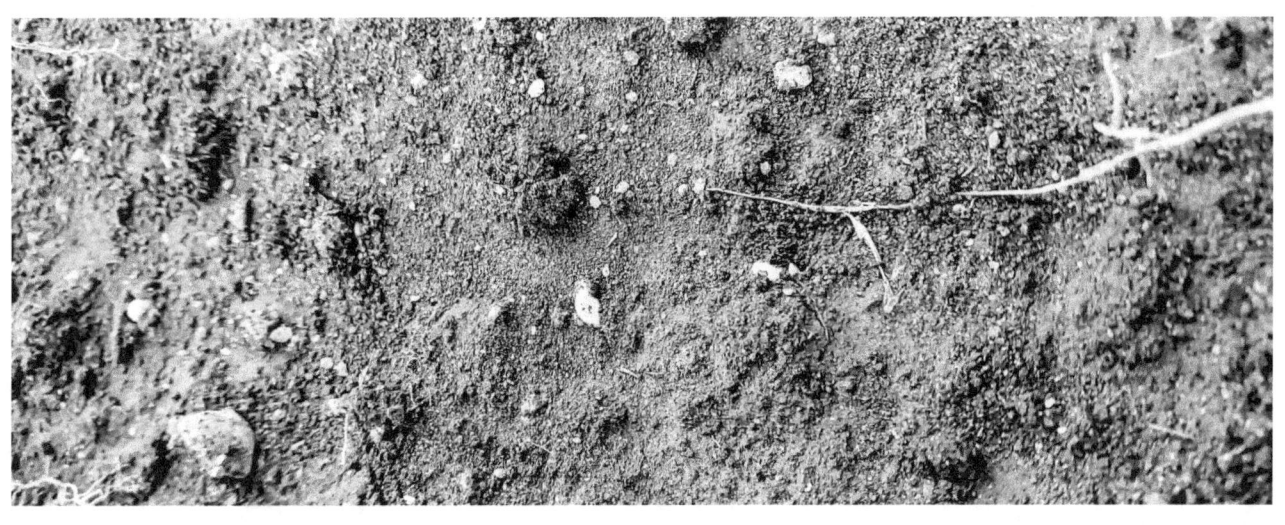

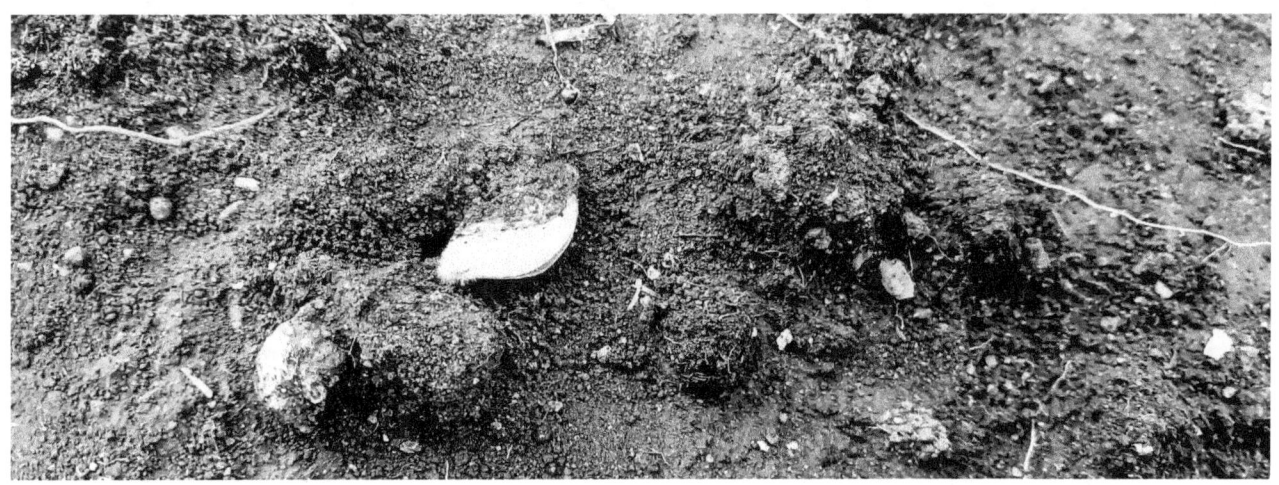

2

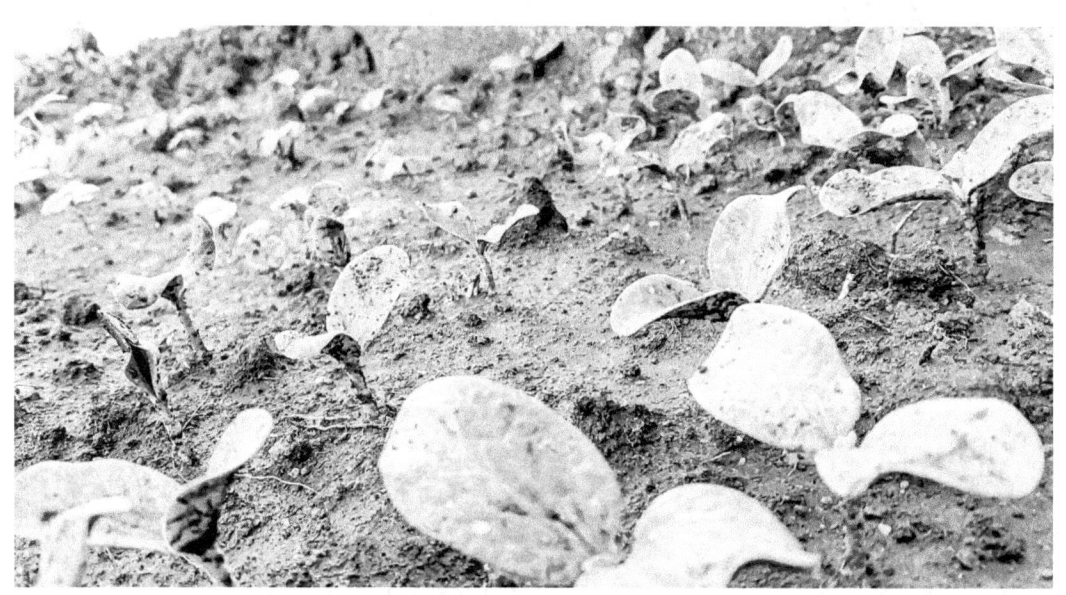

3

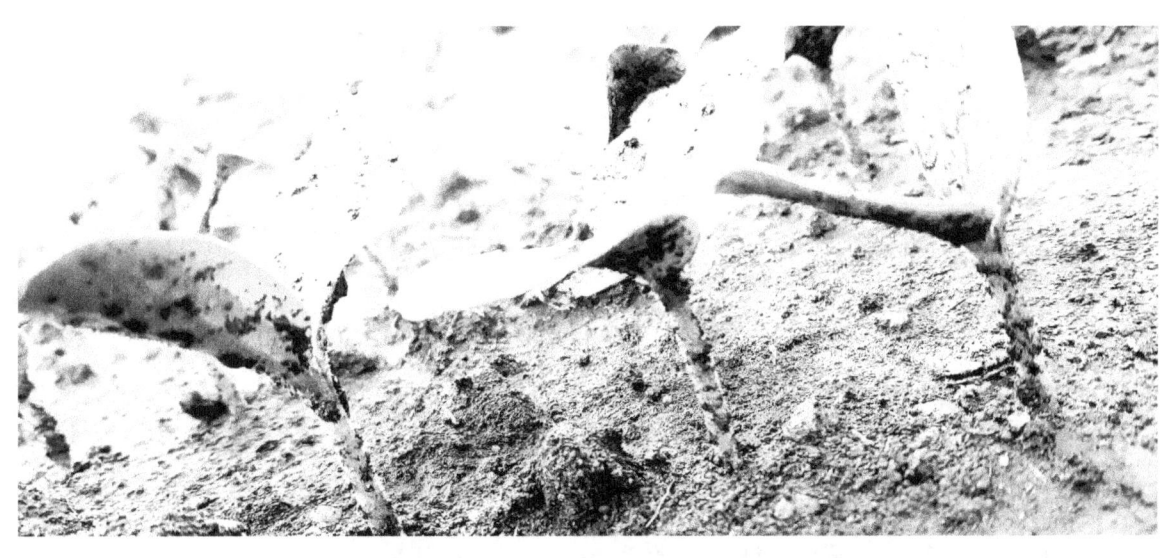

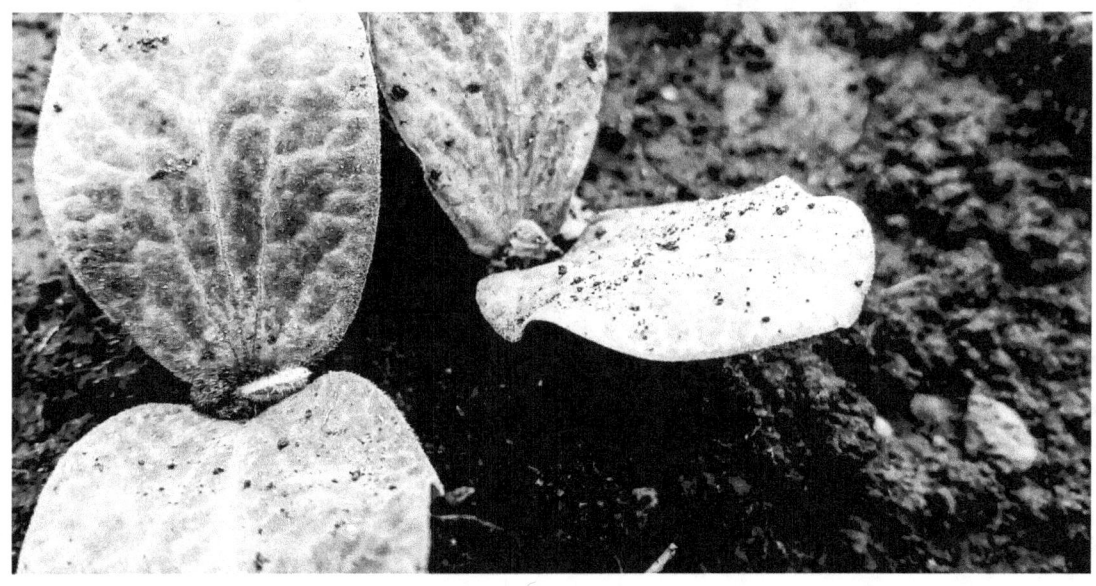

4

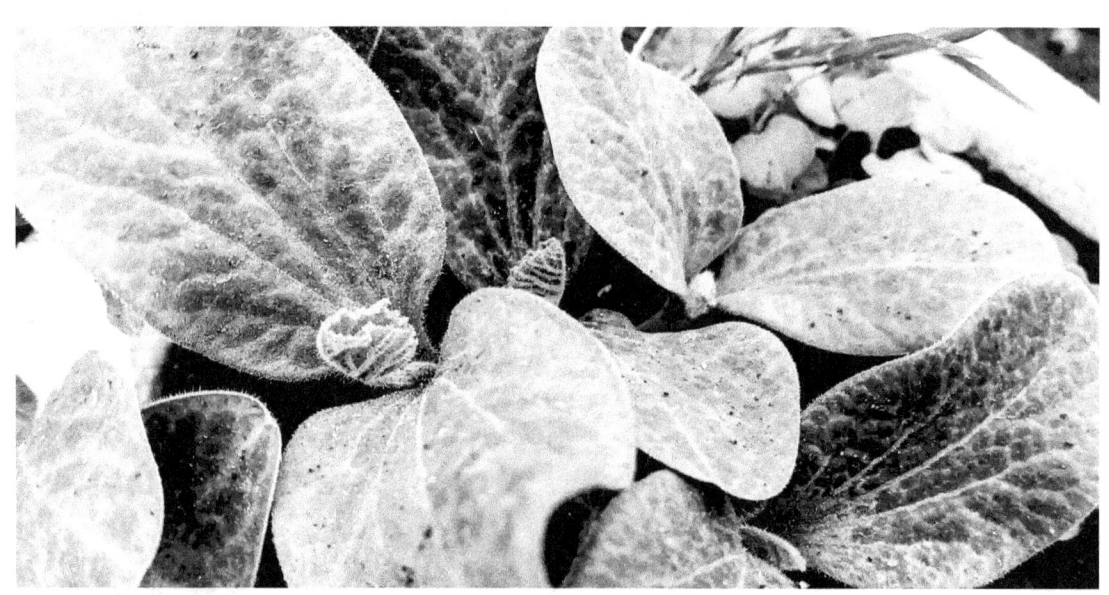

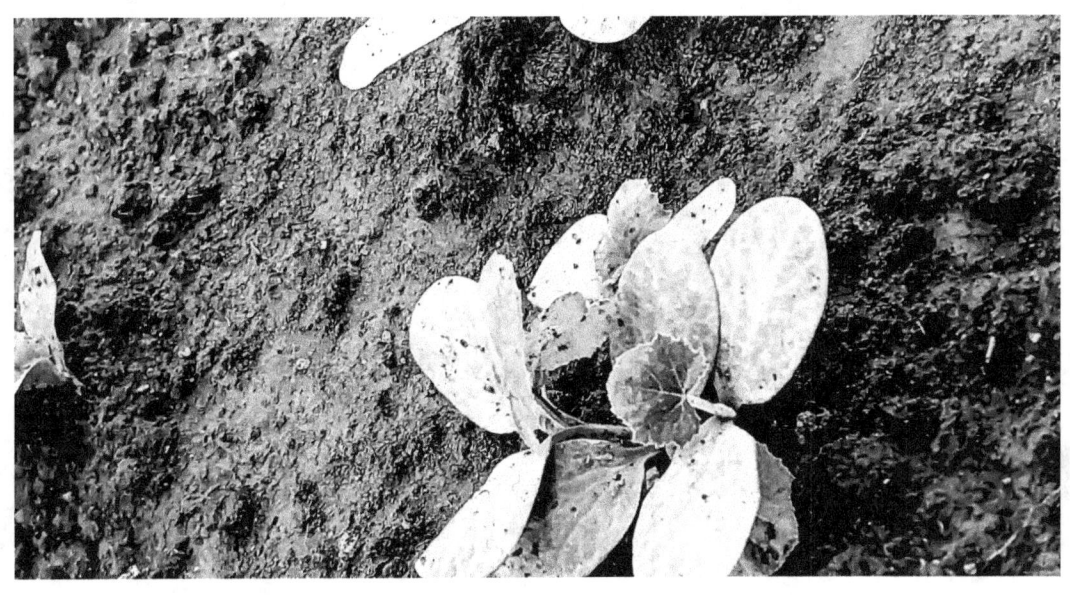

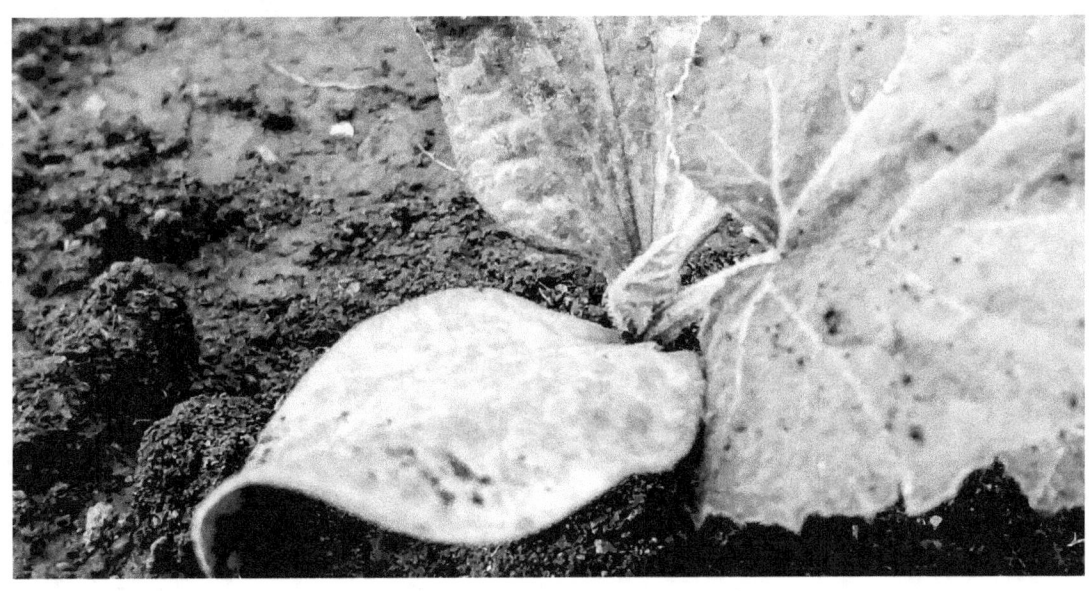

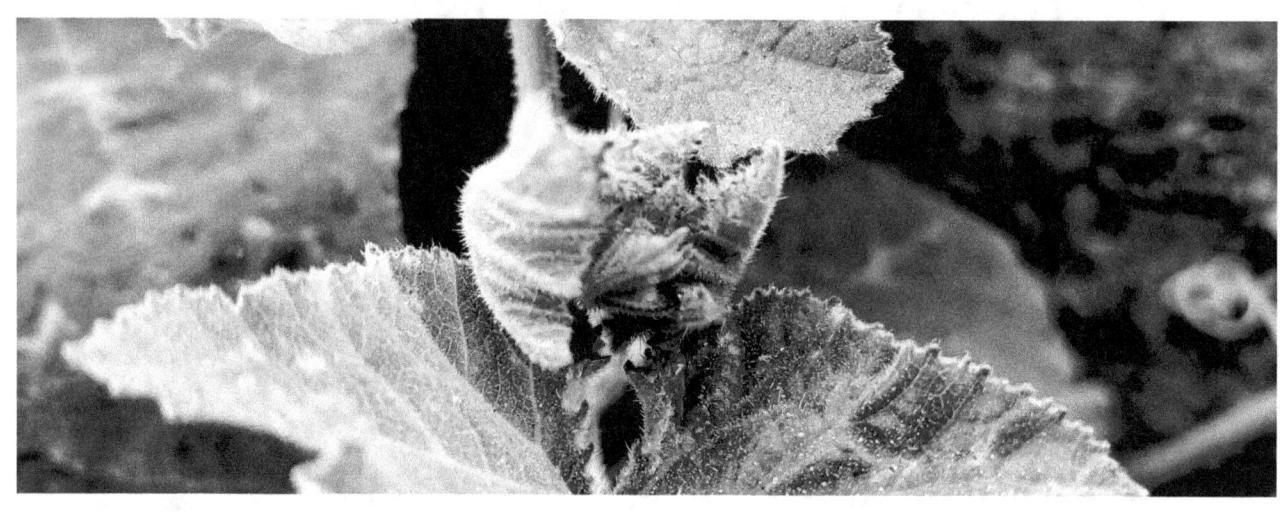

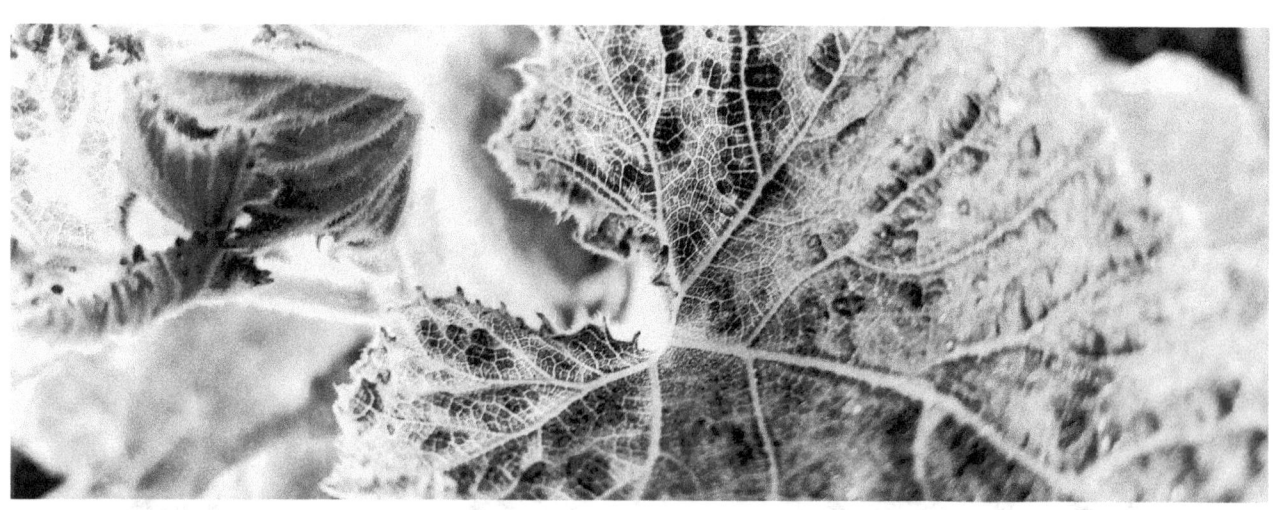

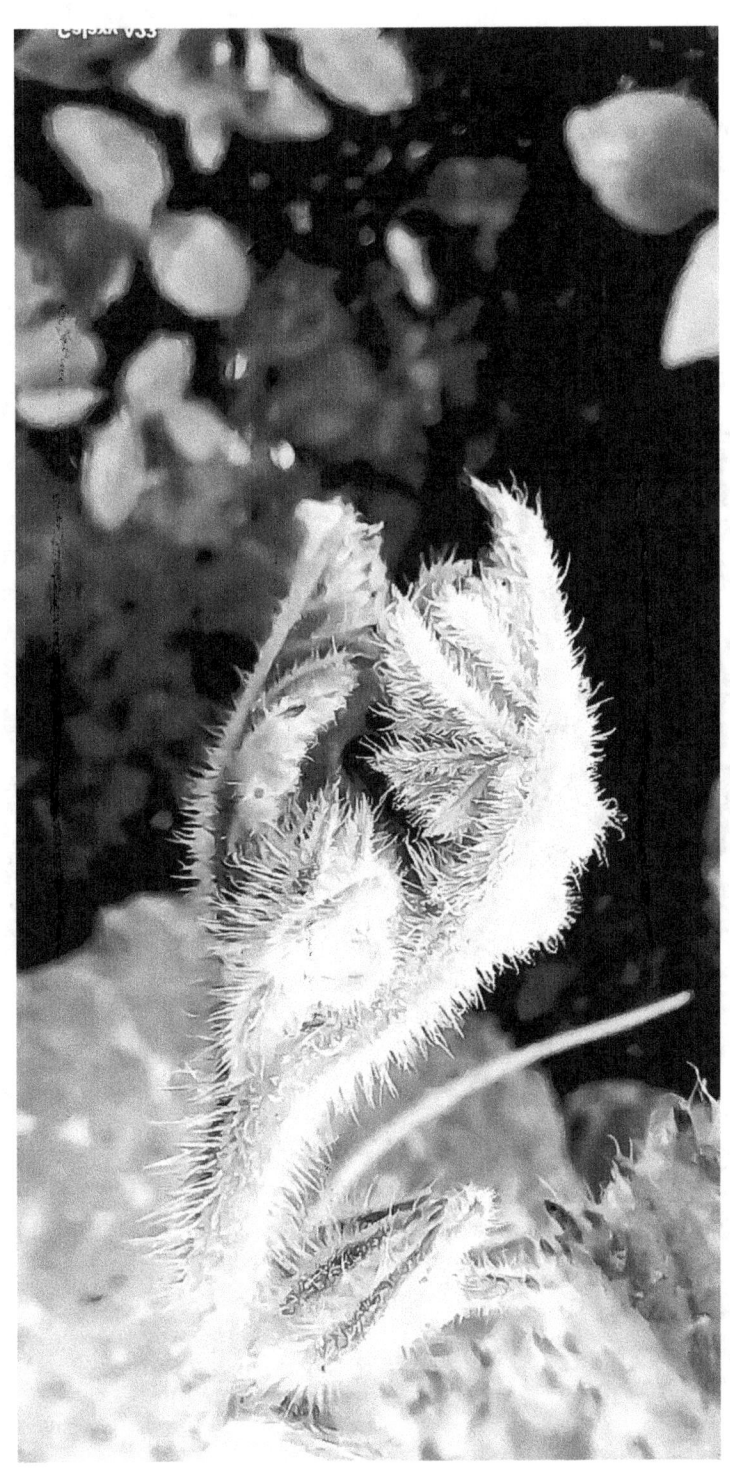

8

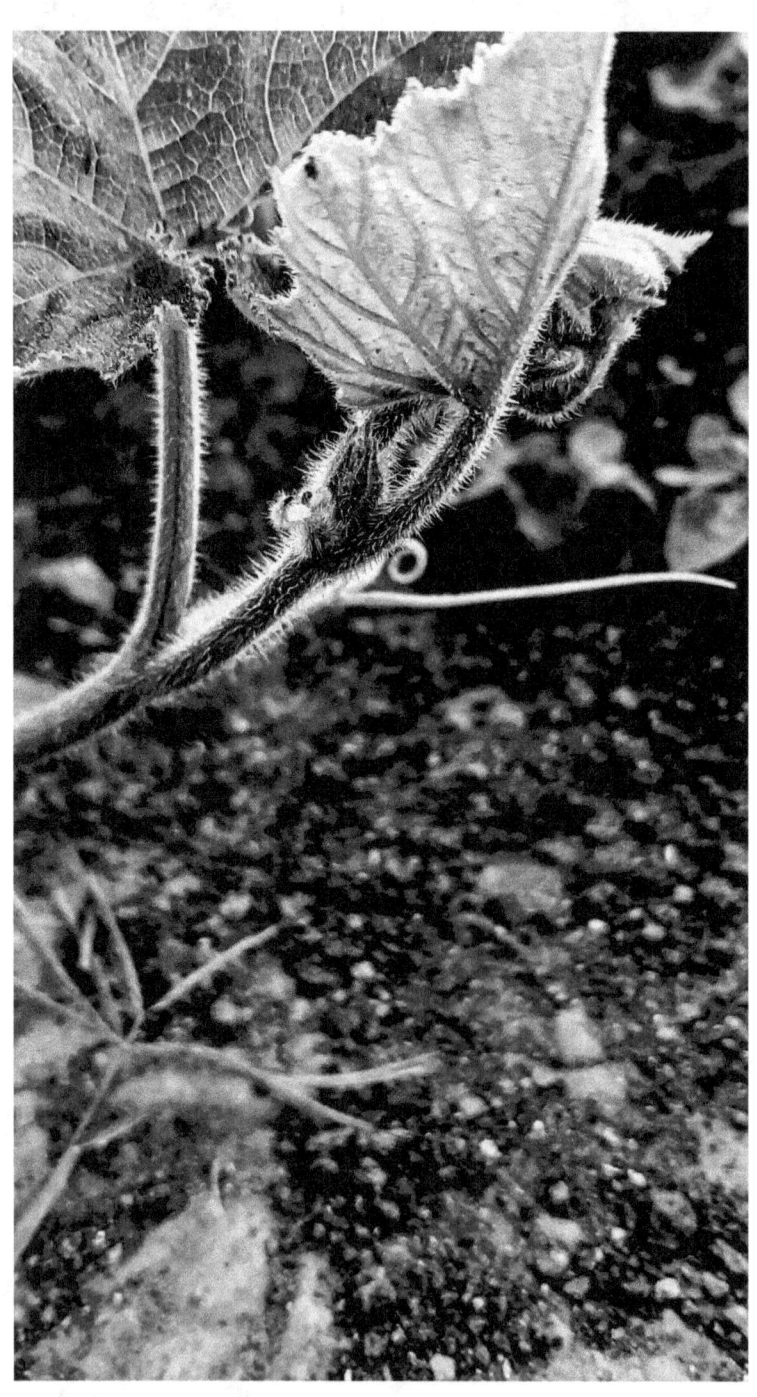

9

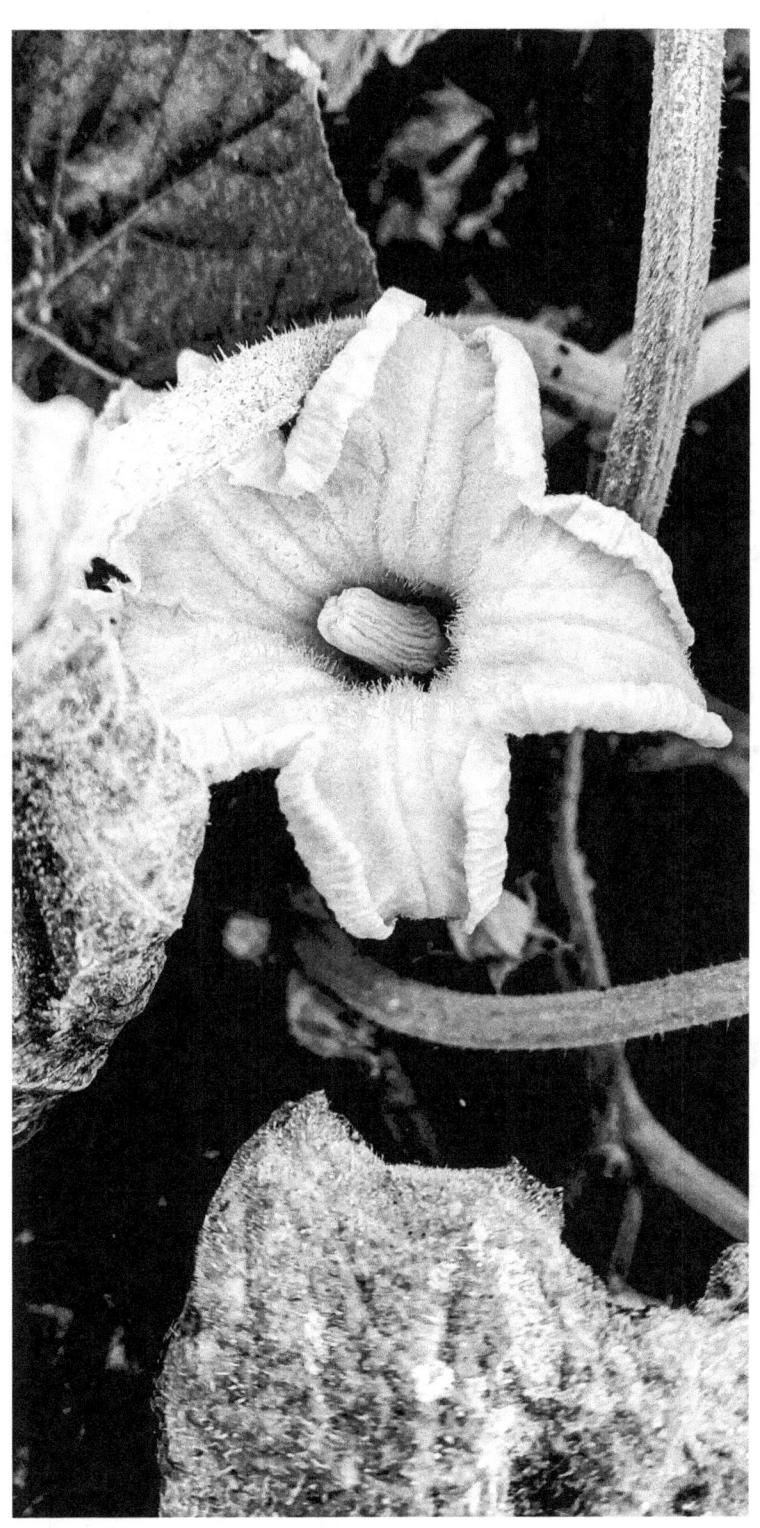

10

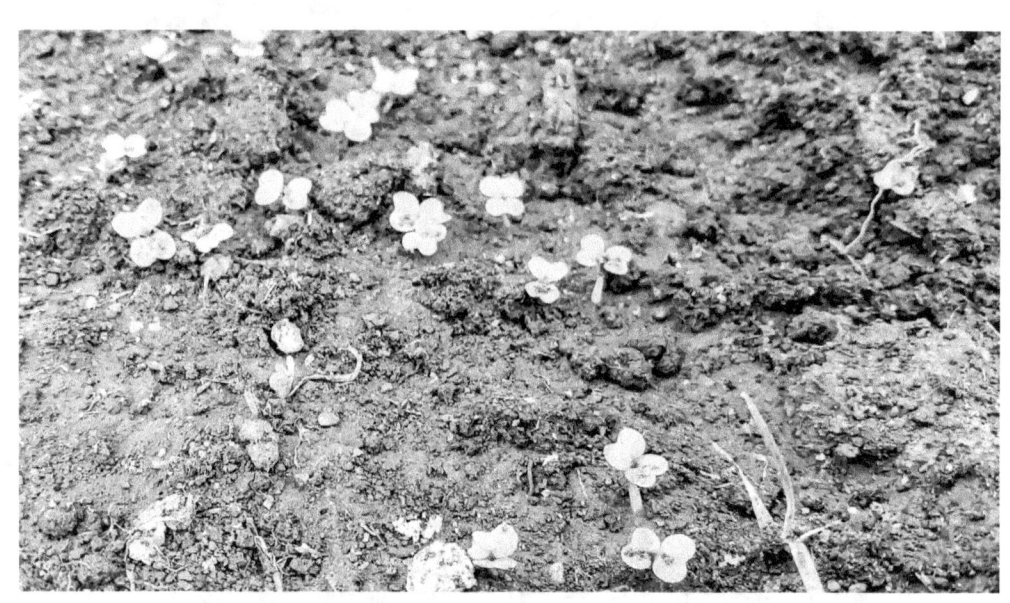

11

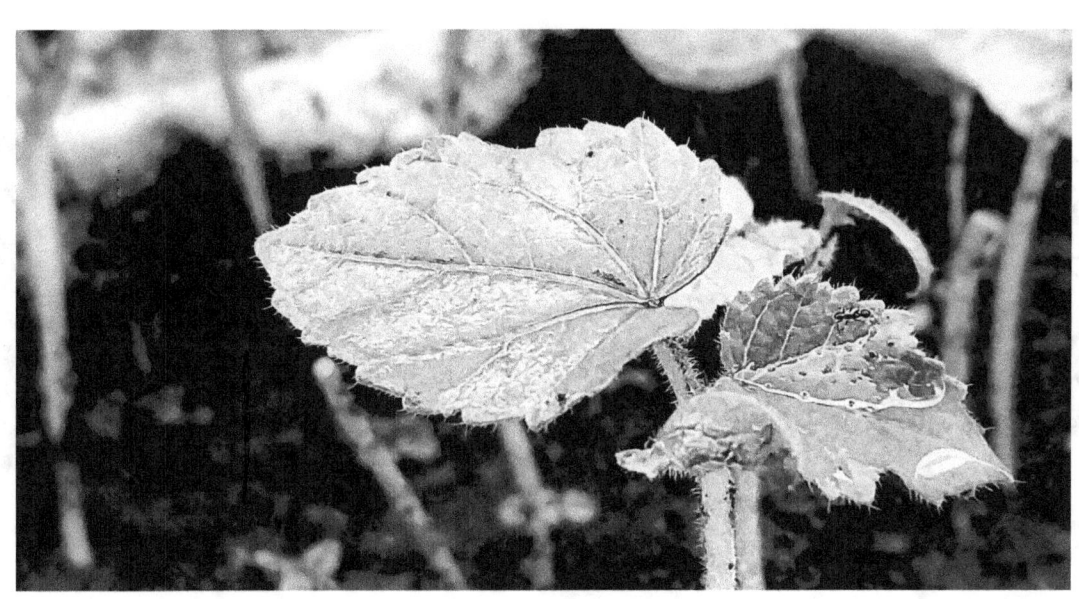

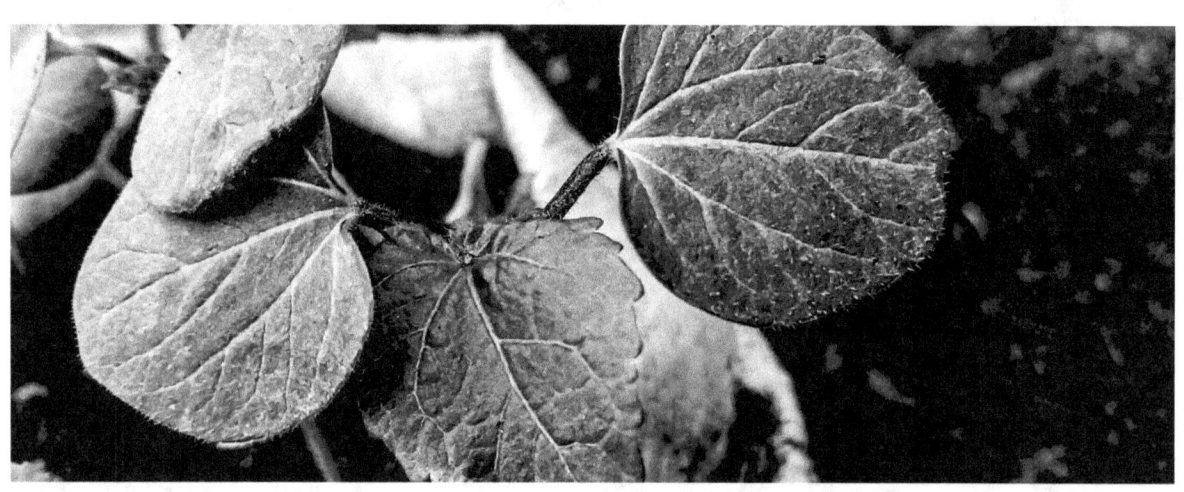

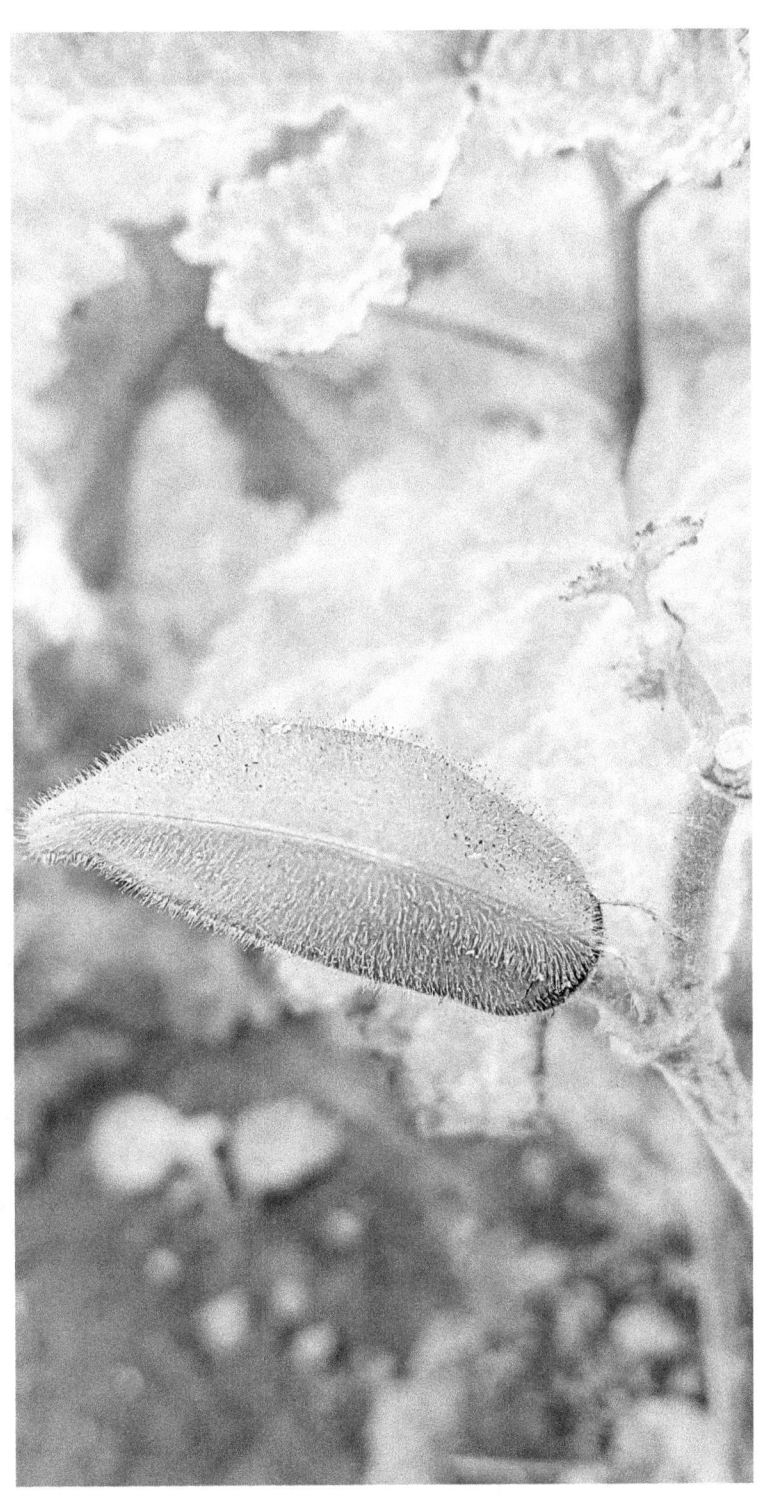

14

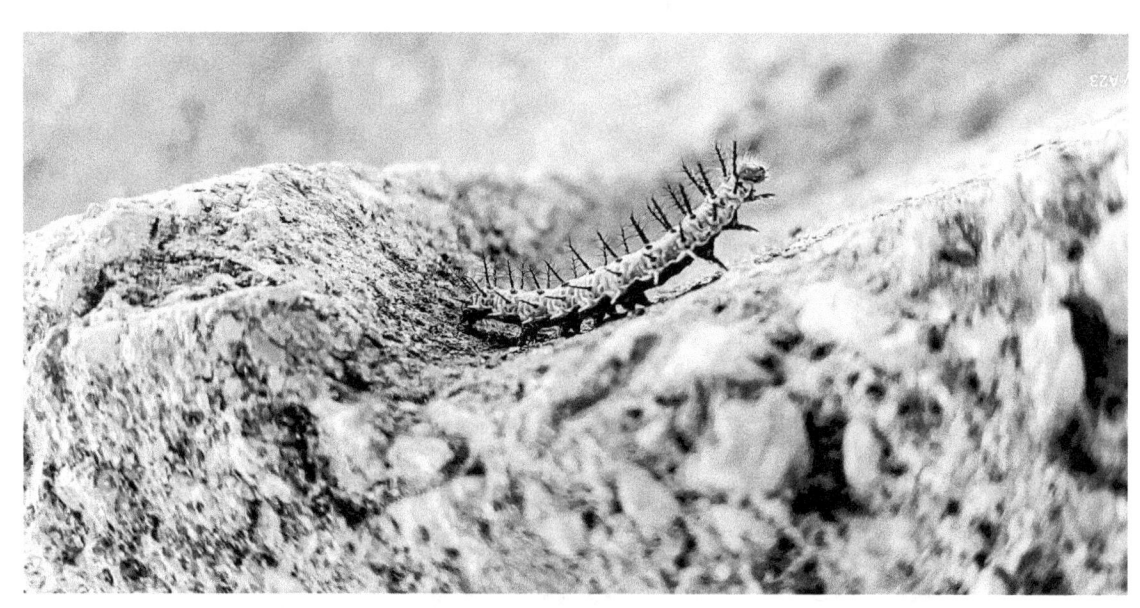

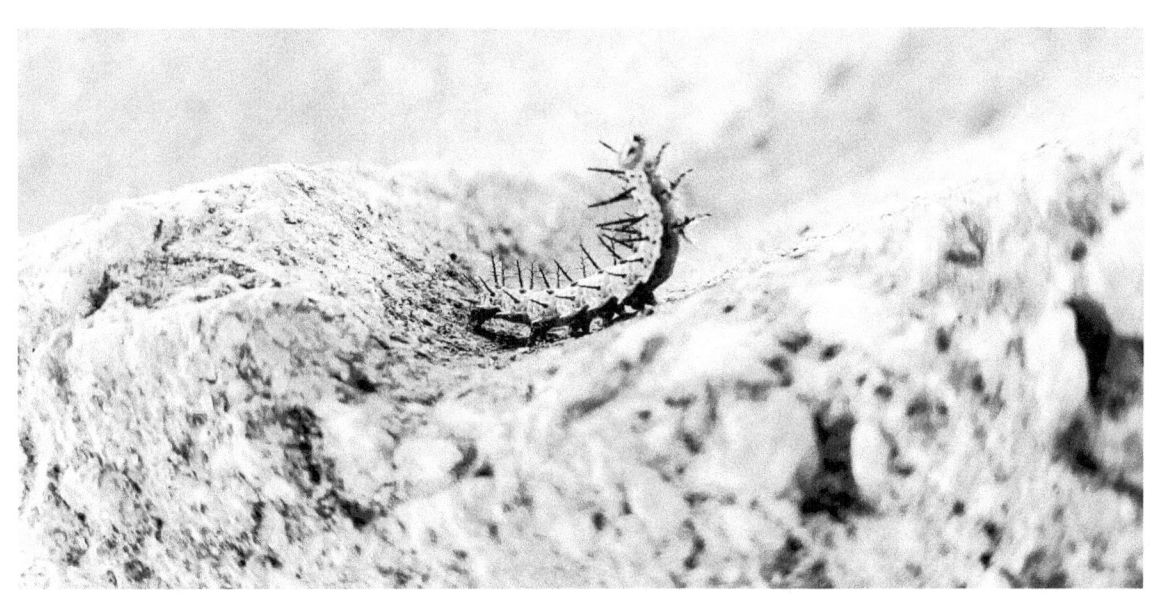

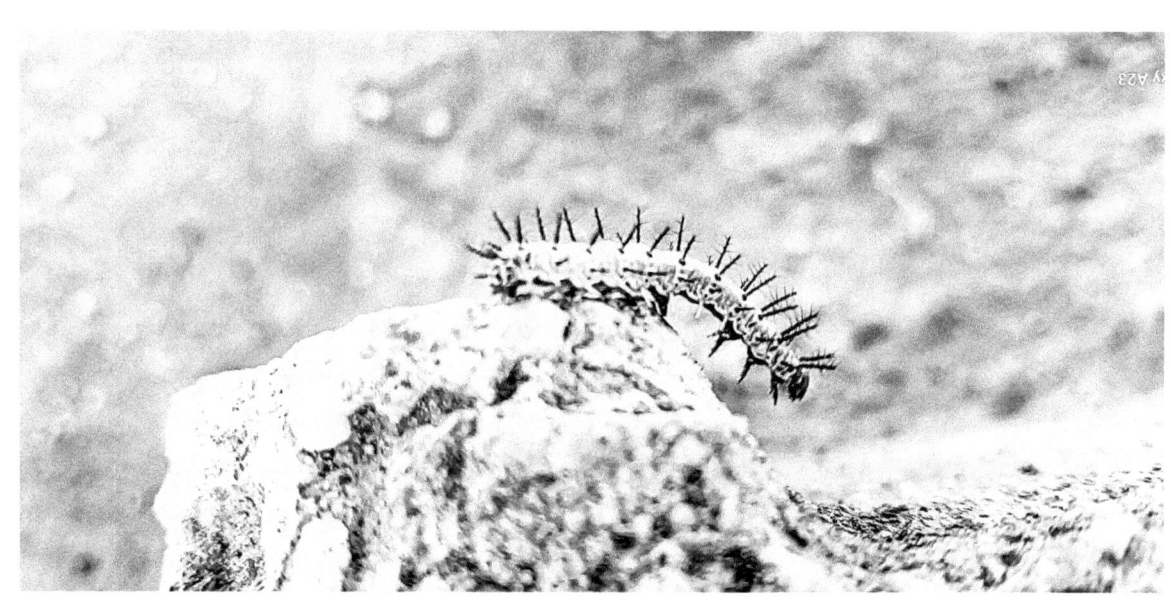

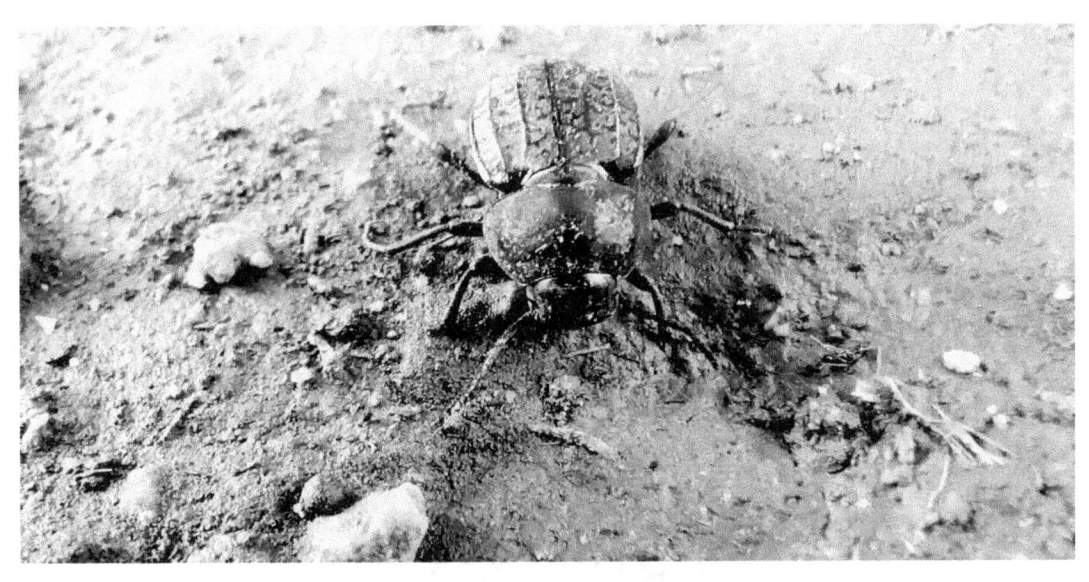

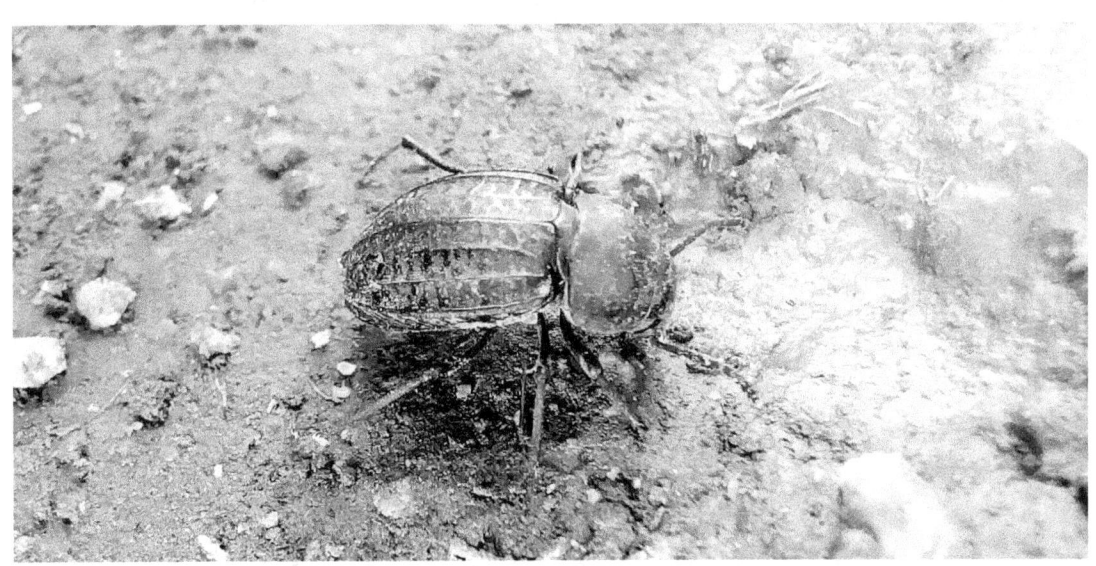

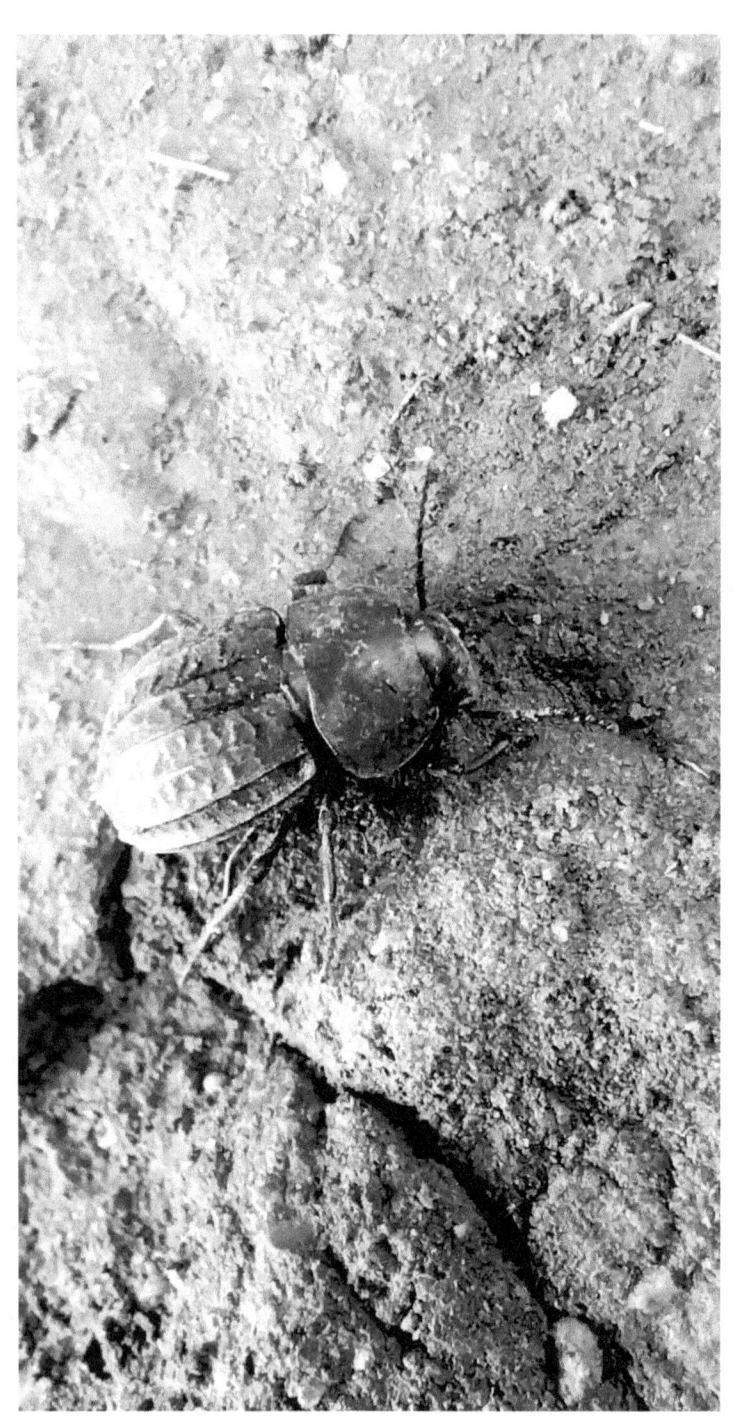

19

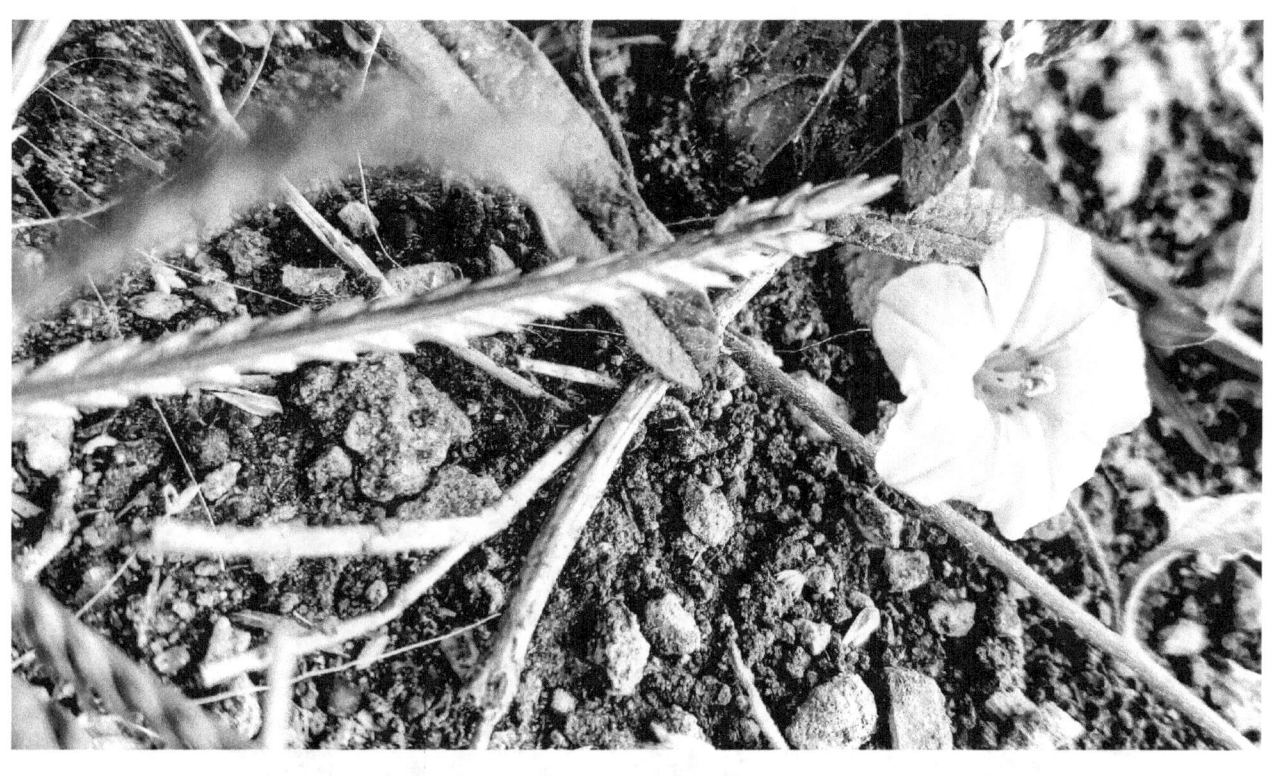

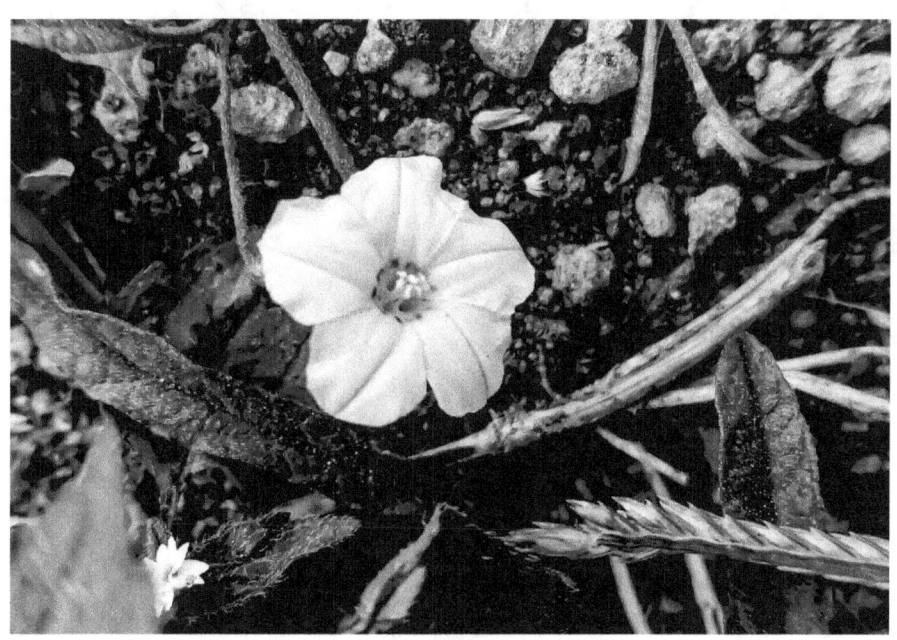

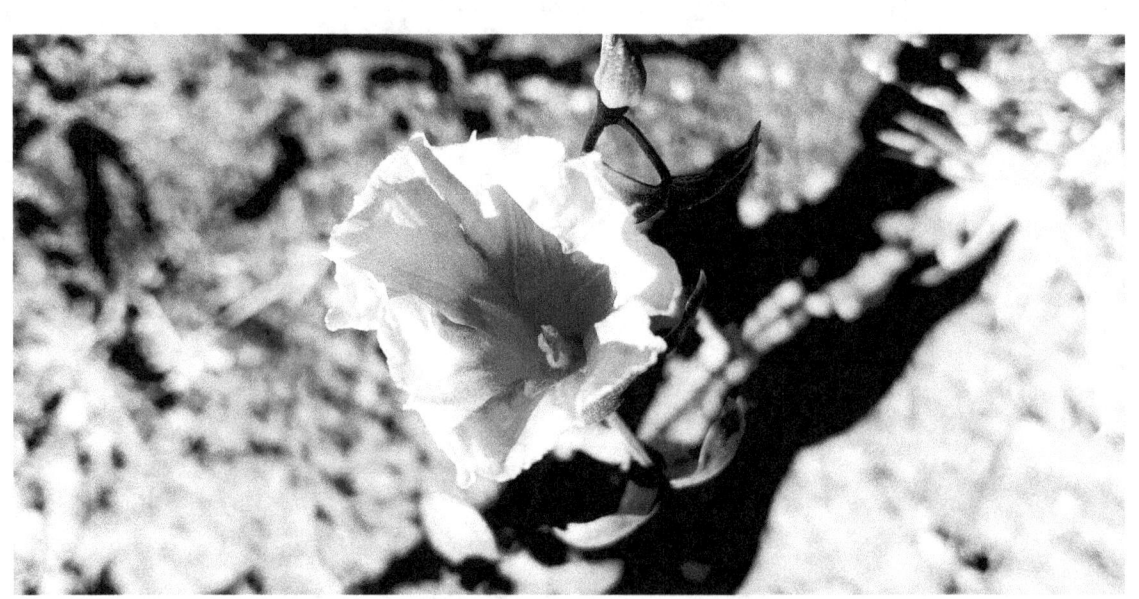

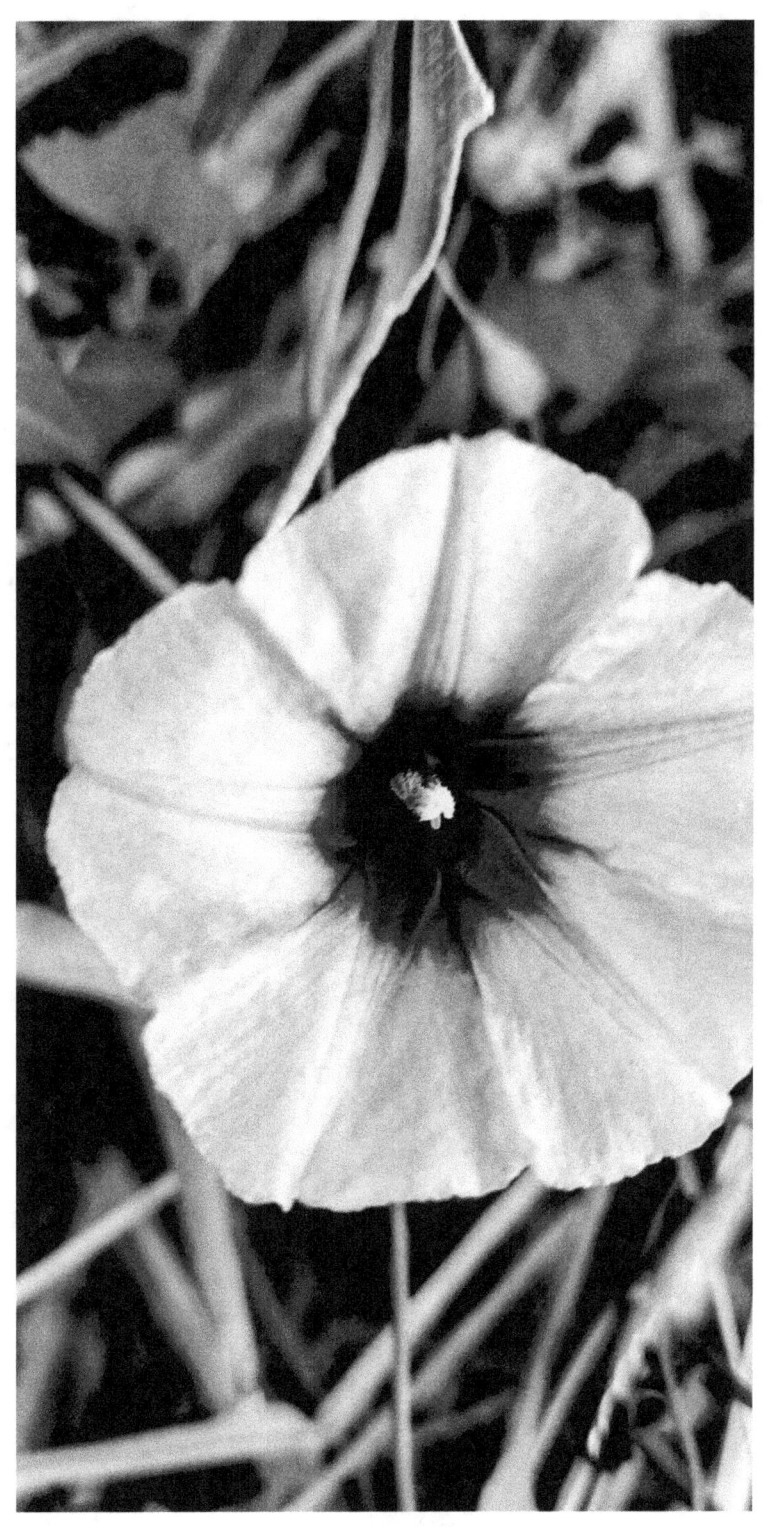

22

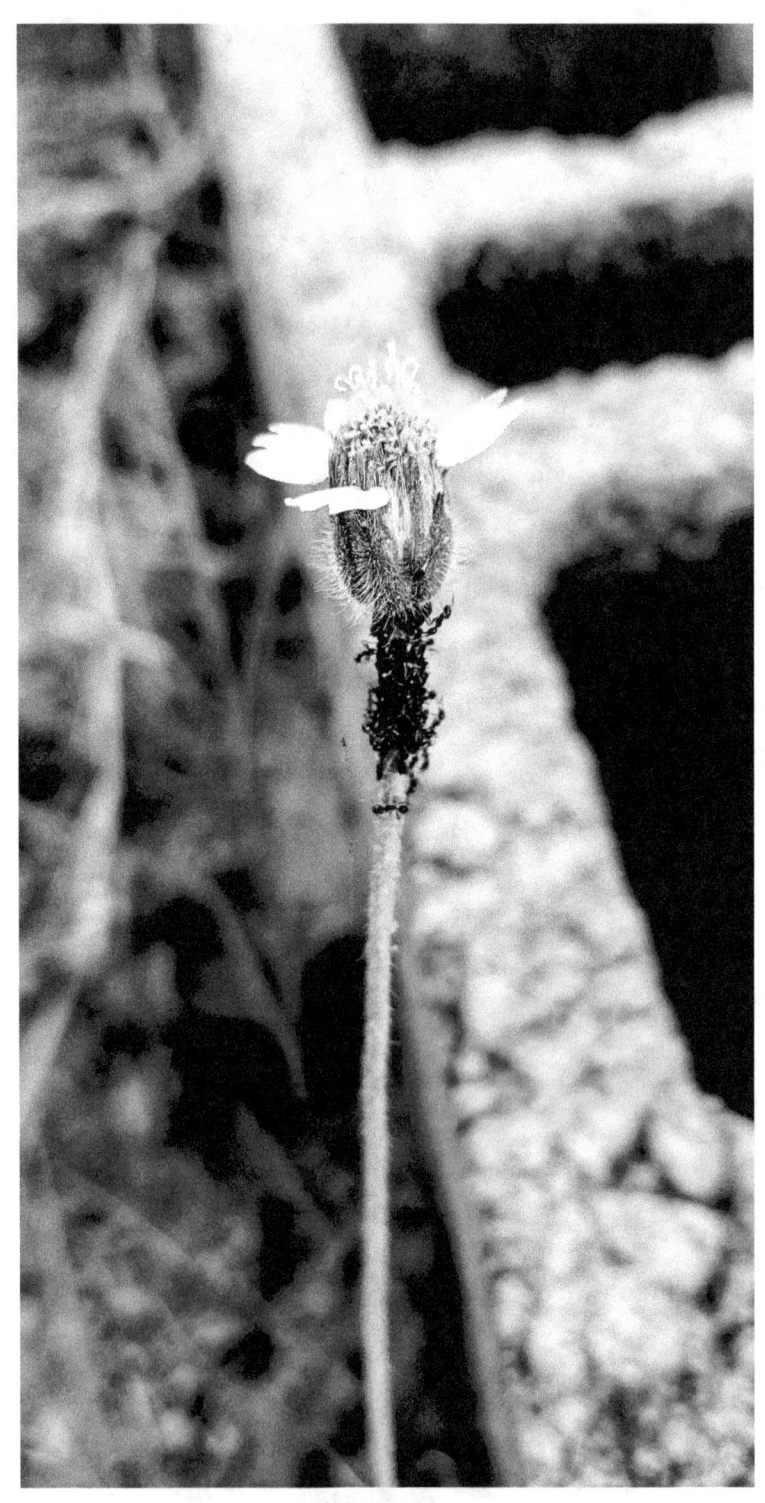

23

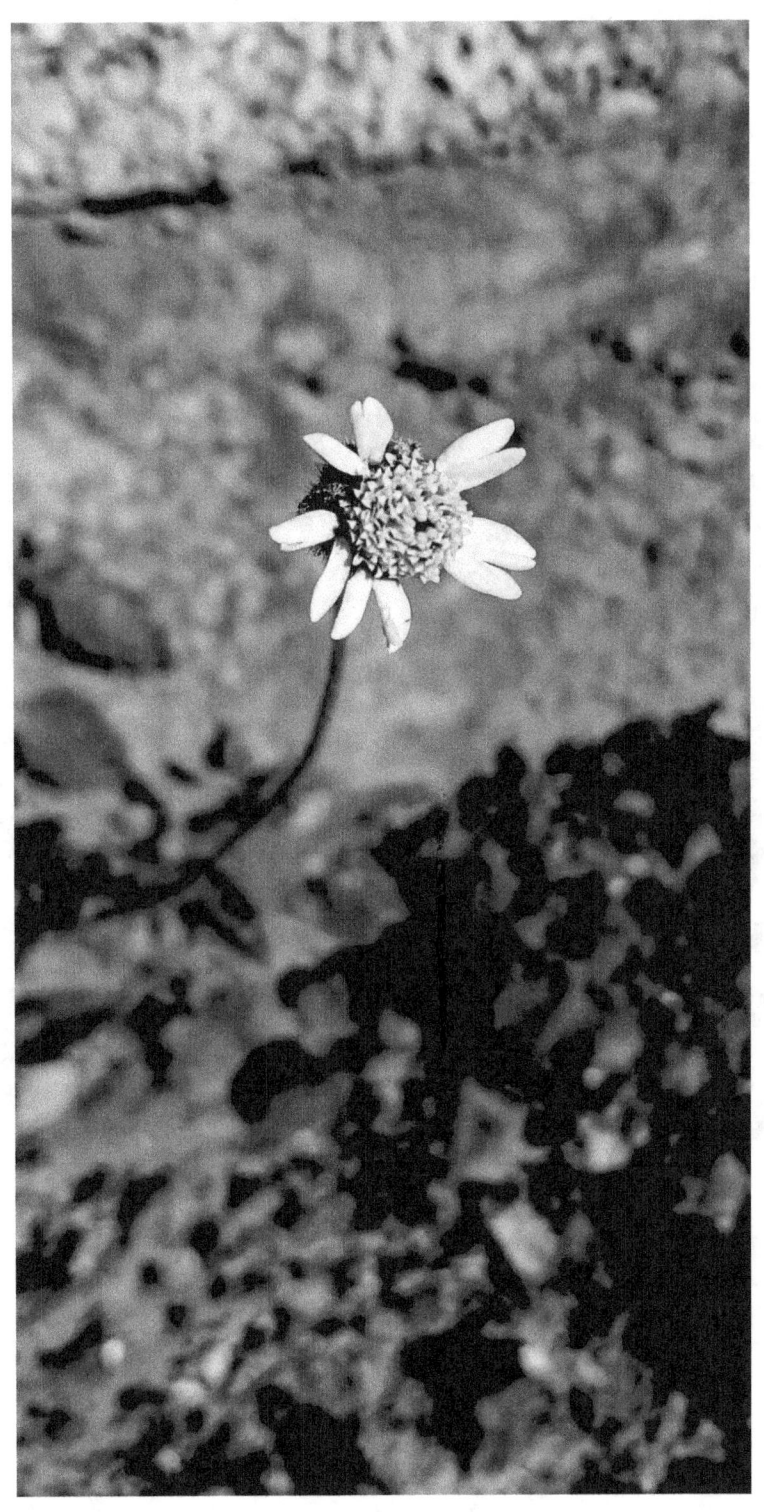

24

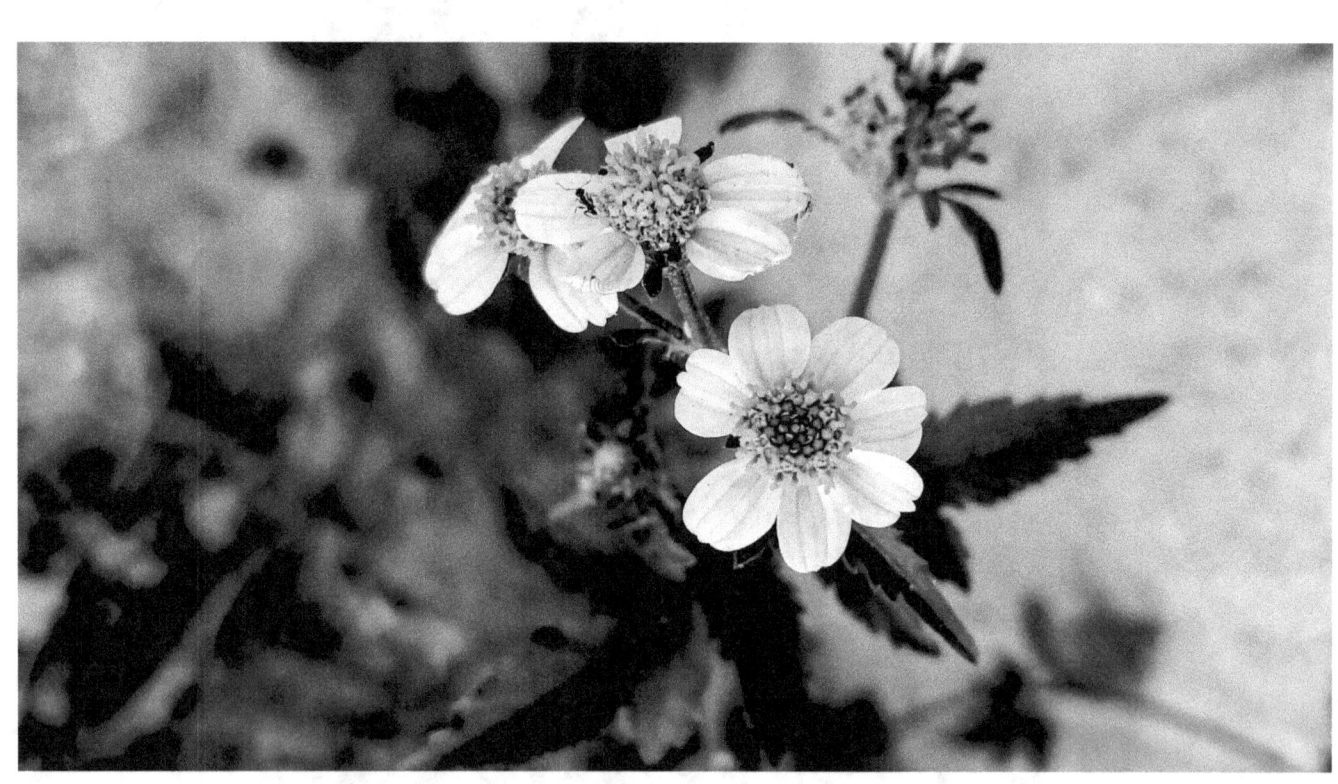

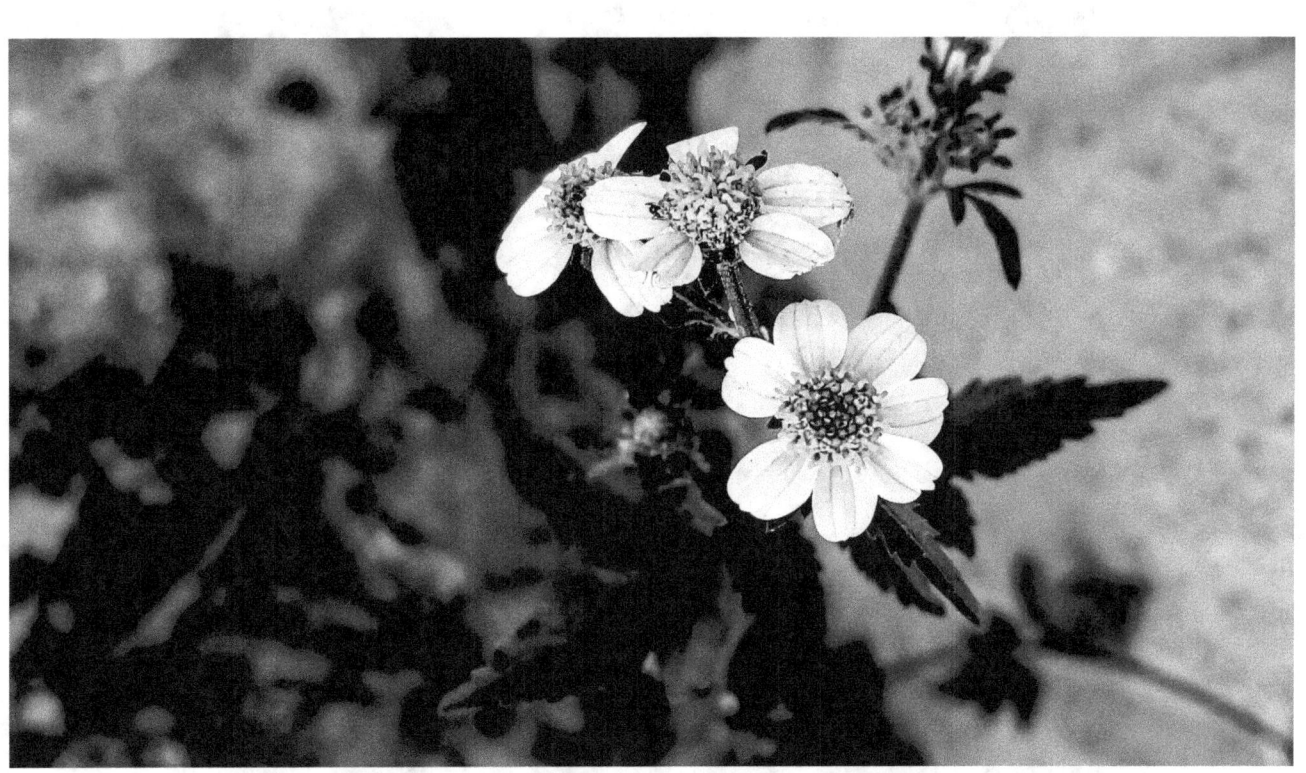

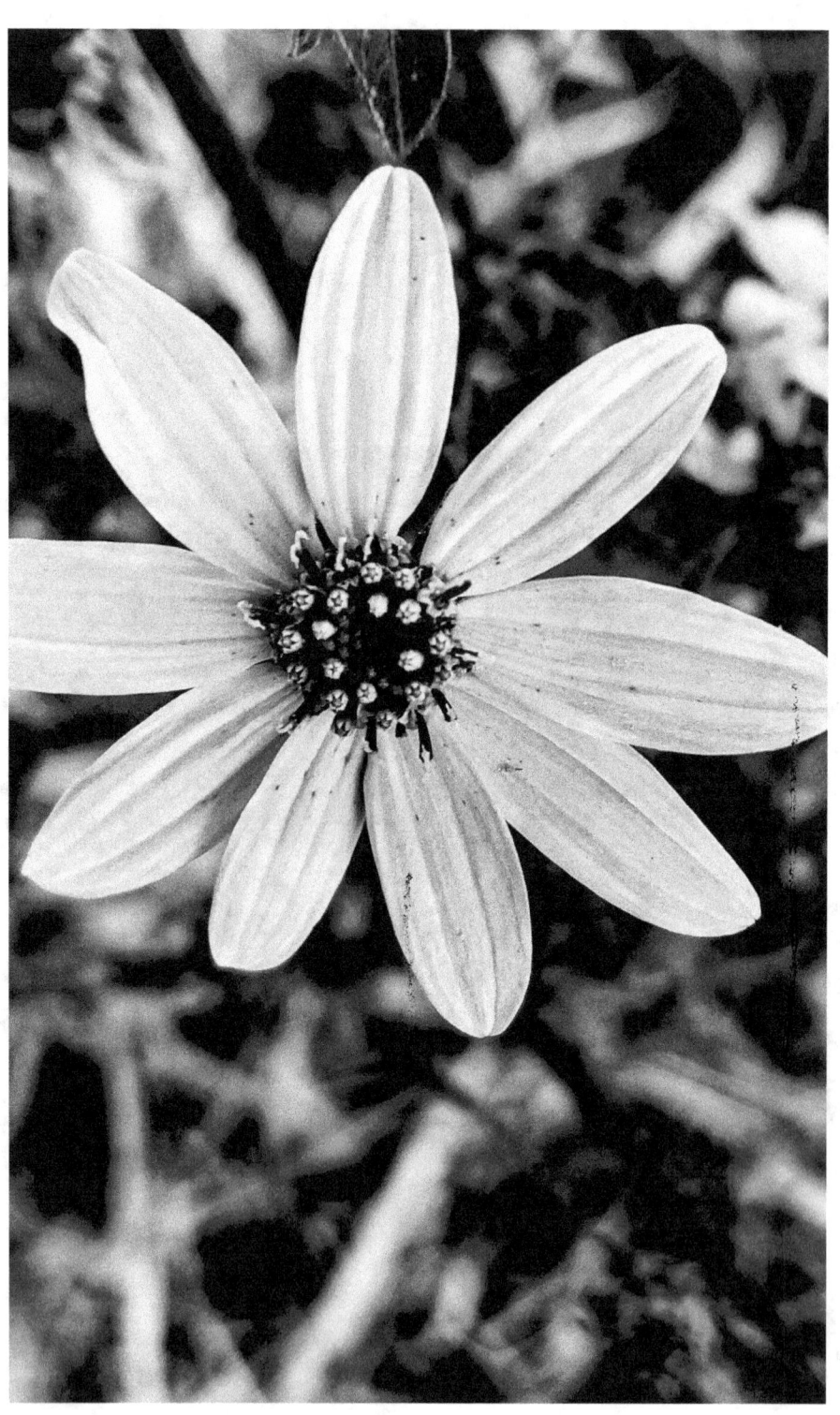

27

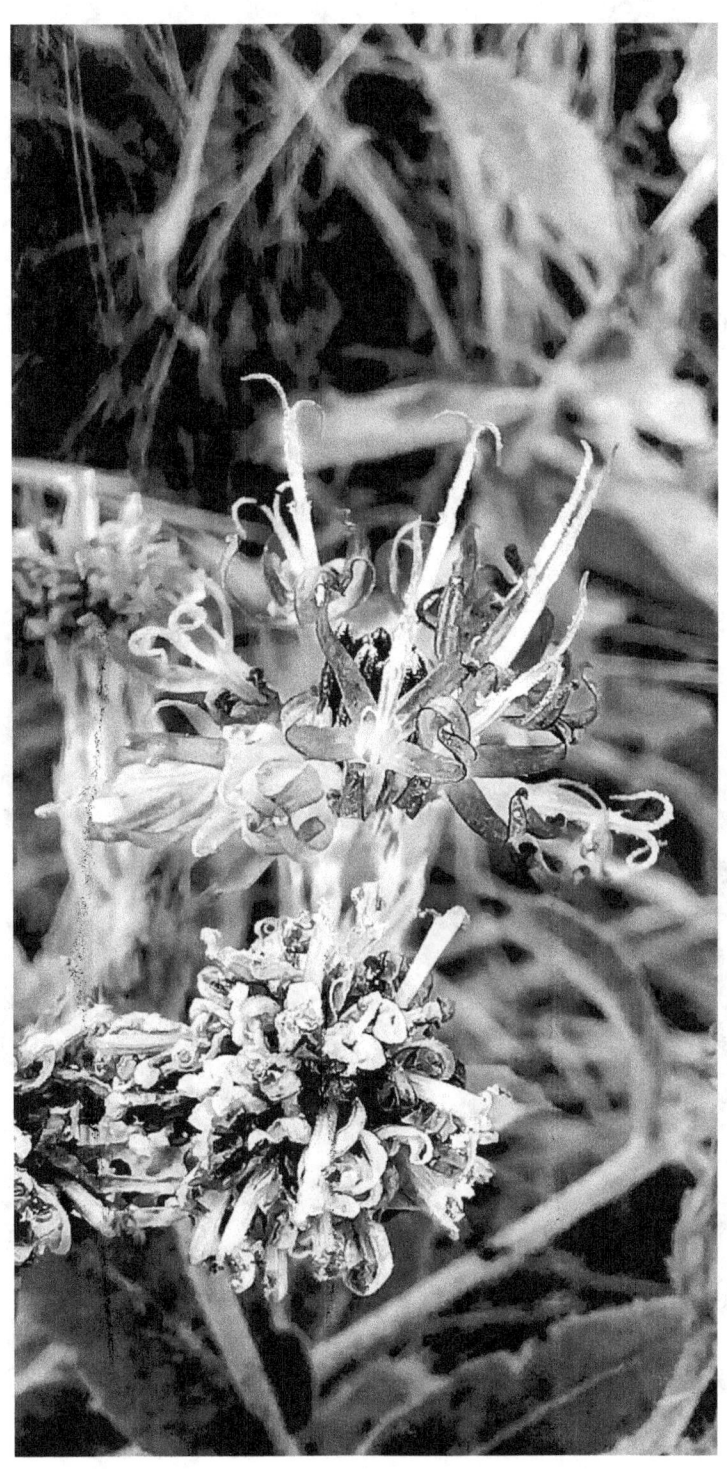

28

29

About The Photos

There are times we look for
simple, beautiful and
meaningful things from afar. If
we stopped for a moment to
look with our eyes right where
we are, we'd see it.
All the photos in this book
were taken from and around
our small backyard garden, on
a piece of land that was
previously occupied by only
trees and grass on farm lands a
short distance on the outskirts
of Zambia's capital city,
Lusaka.

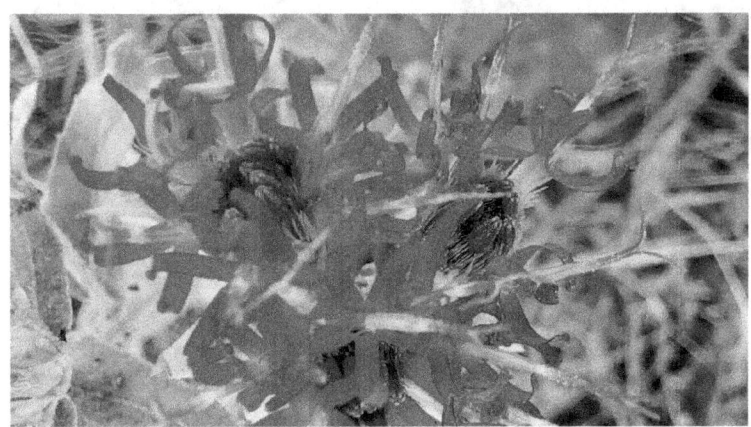

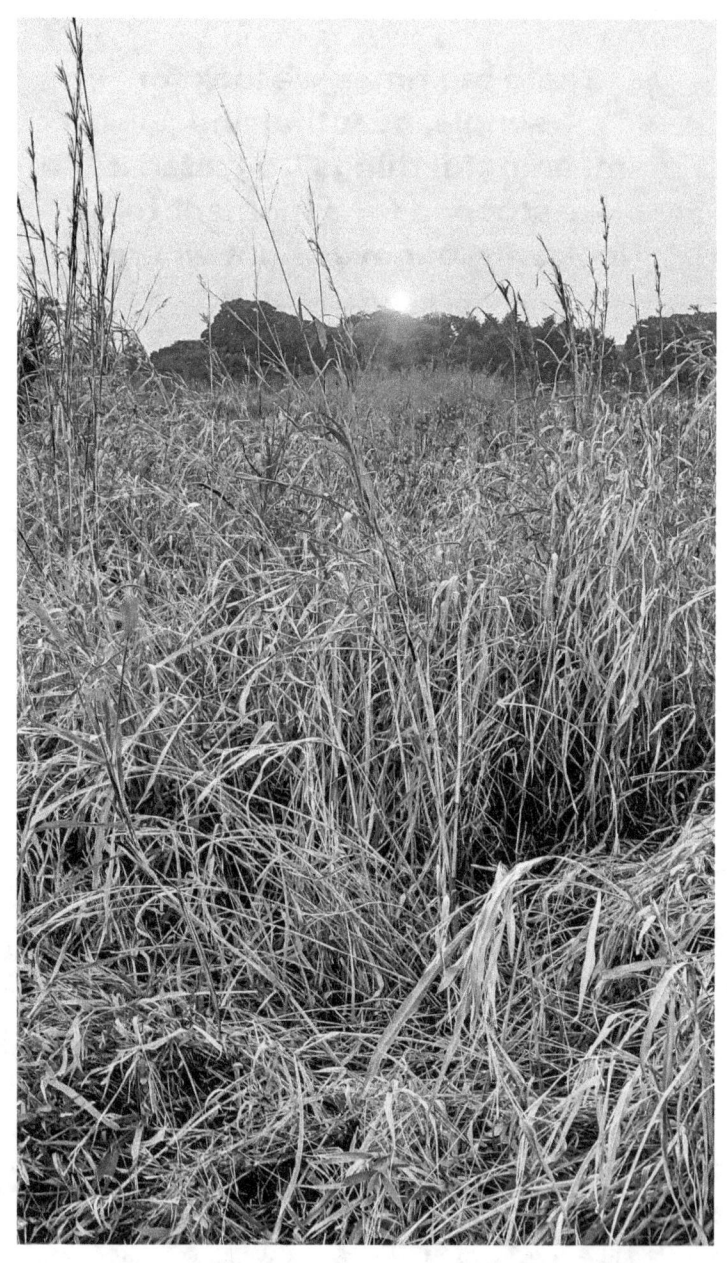

Not The End, Just the beginning.

31